two-hour
window
treatments

two-hour
window
treatments

Linda Durbano
Marni Kissel
Mechelle Christian

Sterling Publishing Co. Inc. New York

A Sterling/Chapelle Book

Chapelle, Ltd.:

- Owner: Jo Packham
- Editor: Laura Best

- Staff: Areta Bingham, Kass Burchett, Marilyn Goff, Holly Hollingsworth, Susan Jorgensen, Kimberly Maw, Barbara Milburn, Linda Orton, Karmen Quinney, Leslie Ridenour, Cindy Stoeckl, Gina Swapp, Kim Taylor, Sara Toliver, Kristi Torsak

- Photography: Kevin Dilley, Hazen Photography
  Joe Coca, Coca Photography
  Phil Cordova, Cordova Photography

If you have any questions or comments, please contact: Chapelle, Ltd., Inc., P.O. Box 9252, Ogden, UT 84409 (801) 621-2777 • (801) 621-2788 Fax
chapelle@chapelleltd.com   www.chapelleltd.com

Library of Congress Cataloging-in-Publication Data

Durbano, Linda.
    Two-hour window treatments / Linda Durbano, Marni Kissel, Mechelle Christian.
       p. cm.
    Includes index.
    ISBN 0-8069-5801-4 Hardcover
    ISBN 1-4027-0077-6 Paperback

    1. Draperies. 2. Draperies in interior decoration. 3. Valances (Windows) 4. Window shades. I. Kissel, Marni. II. Christian, Mechelle. III. Title.

TT390 D87 2001
747'.5--dc21
                                                                00-053788

10 9 8 7 6 5 4 3 2 1

Published by Sterling Publishing Company, Inc.
387 Park Avenue South, New York, NY 10016
©2001 by Linda Durbano
Distributed in Canada by Sterling Publishing
C/o Canadian Manda Group, One Atlantic Avenue, Suite 105 Toronto, Ontario, Canada M6K 3E7
Distributed in Australia by Capricorn Link (Australia) Pty Ltd.
P.O. Box 704, Windsor, NSW 2756, Australia

Printed and Bound in China
All Rights Reserved

Sterling ISBN 0-8069-5801-4 Hardcover
        ISBN 1-4027-0077-6 Paperback

This book is dedicated to all of the
fathers in our lives: Lyman, Dave, Garth,
Greg, Keith, and especially Tom.

tableofcontents

thebeginning

Linda, second from left, has been happily married to Teresa's, Marni's, and Mechelle's father for 23 years.

This book is intended to put enjoyment into designing. If you learn a little about style and interior design, you are ahead of the game. If you are able to create some fun and decorative window coverings in a short amount of time, we have achieved our goal and you have made your home more livable and enjoyable.

Whether you are looking for elegance, retro, casual, or chic, we have touched on a variety of window treatment designs. We have included a number of quick and easy projects that can be completed in minutes. We have also explained a number of more sophisticated ideas for window coverings requiring a little more time.

If you want to open up a window and let the sunshine in, you are reading the right book. If you want to close out the ghastly brick wall outside your apartment window, you are also reading the right book. Whatever you are after, this is a great time to begin.

We loved compiling this book for you. Though our interests vary, we always enjoy getting together and sharing ideas. We have worked together professionally on a number of decorating projects, and some of our clients' homes are featured in this book.

Aside from designing for Chapelle, Ltd., Linda Cassity Durbano devotes the majority of her efforts as Vice President of Marketing for the Verde Canyon Railroad in Clarkdale, Arizona. She and her husband, Dave, also breed and raise paint and quarter horses at Snowy Range Ranch in Laramie, Wyoming.

Linda and Dave have six children, nine grandchildren, and three dogs—Boomer, Bo, and Sergio.

Though Marni Kissel's first love is decorating and design, she focuses much of her attention on operating her father's railroad businesses—working side-by-side with her husband Greg. They have three children, and reside in Utah with their two black labradors, Cade and Coal.

Mechelle Christian spends her time raising her daughter, Carly, in Ogden, Utah. Aside from interior design, Mechelle actively markets for Garth Widdison Motor Sports, who specializes in top-fuel dragsters.

We have enjoyed working together on this project to bring you a wide variety of window treatments. Now it is your turn to create and enjoy!

windowshavetwosides

I remember, I remember,
The house where I was born,
The little window where the sun
Came peeping in at morn.
— Thomas Hood

The first and foremost thing to remember when designing and placing a window covering is that it is visible from two sides: inside your home and outside your house. Especially when a house has multiple windows visible from the same side, it is essential that all windows reflect a camaraderie of design. Always be conscientious of the exterior look of the window dressing, as well as how it plays indoors.

Light,
God's eldest daughter,
Is a principal beauty
In a building.
— Thomas Fuller

lightandview

When designing a house or building, an architect uses window placement to enhance the exterior architecture of the structure while considering the impact it will have on the interior of the home.

Occasionally, the view is spectacular enough to require no other window adornment, so the style of windows, number of windows, and size of windows become more important in the initial architectural design.

The same should apply when designing window treatments. Keeping in mind the two elementary functions of a window—*light and view*—use a window treatment that intensifies what you expect from the window—sometimes more and sometimes less.

Improvisation is too good to
leave to chance.
— Paul Simon

gettingstarted

Choosing the right materials for your window will make all of the difference in how happy you will be when your window treatment is completed. Whether you choose vintage fabrics, antique treasures, presewn fabric panels, or flea market finds, be certain pieces are compatible with the room's interior scheme, especially when using materials which are not normally used for window treatments.

Measure the window accurately to be certain your choices fit the window and adjacent walls. Draperies can be either sill-length, apron-length, or floor-length. For good proportion, valances and swags are often one-fifth the window length or the completed treatment. Cascades are often one- to two-thirds the length of the window. Avoid dividing the window treatment in half visually.

• When measuring, use a steel tape measure or wooden yard stick.

• Hang rod before measuring. To determine the finished length of the window treatment, measure from the top of the curtain rod or mounting board to the desired length of the window treatment; if the window treatment will have a heading above the rod, add the length of the heading to this measurement.

If making treatments for several windows in the same room, measure and record the measurements for each window separately, even if they appear to be the same size.

• For shutters, flat curtains, and shades, use the window width, measure either from outside or inside of the casing. If the treatment goes inside the casing, measure across at three different points and use the widest measurement.

- Depending on preferred fullness, plan on 1½ to 2½ times the area covered, when purchasing fabric or premade panels.

- Depending on the thickness and size of fabric, use the following measurements as a guideline:
3"–6" for hems
2"–3" for side hems
½" seam allowance

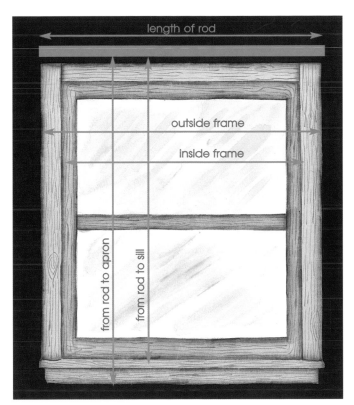

- When creating a valance, it is better to make a valance too long than too short.

- Specific amounts of supplies are not always listed in the projects. Read through all instructions before measuring and purchasing supplies. Take any measurements as described in instructions.

- You may wish to purchase 10–20% extra of the fabrics and trims for insurance against flaws or errors. Coordinating pillows, napkins, or place mats may be made from any excess fabrics or trims.

- To lower hems, add double the desired hem to finished length. For medium weight fabrics, add 8" to the length for a 4" double hem on floor-length curtains or draperies. For sheer and lightweight fabrics, a deeper double hem of 5"–6" may be used. On short curtains or valances, use a 1"–3" double hem.

For rod pockets with no heading, add an amount equal to the diameter of the rod plus ½" to turn under and ¼"–1" ease. The amount of ease depends on the thickness of the fabric and the size of the rod. Lightweight fabrics require less ease, rod pockets for large rods require more. For rod pockets with headings, use the formula for a rod pocket, adding to it an amount twice the depth of the heading.

- Pattern repeat: Prints must match across the width of the panels. Measure the distance between motifs, and add that amount to the cut length of each panel.

It is better to be beautiful than to be good.
But . . . it is better to be good than to be ugly.
— Oscar Wilde

fabrics, trims, and everything inbetween

Almost anything, as you will see in this book, can be used to decorate, enhance, or cover a window.

• Search for fabulous vintage fabrics, including old curtains, tablecloths, linens, or lace.

• Scour the attic or garage for family heirlooms or collectibles.

• Use mementos from vacations, hobbies, or sports.

• Visit markets and antique sales for unique objects and art suitable for hanging.

• Watch for premade fabric panels available in discount and variety stores.

• Be certain your window reflects who you are and what makes you happy.

Tab-top or tie-top curtains have open headings with loops, ties, or rings to show off decorative curtain rods. Tab-top curtains can be made in several tiers as café curtains, or as a pair of panels. With the exception of the heading, tab-top curtains are made like basic rod-pocket curtains. Measure curtain rod and estimate fabric requirements. Use the standard 1" side and 3" doubled bottom hem allowances, but add just ⅝" for a

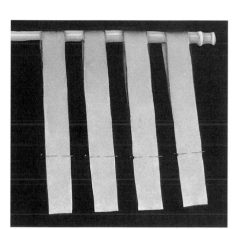

seam allowance on the top. To detemine how much extra fabric to allow for the loops and facing on the curtain heading, draw a full-sized pattern for the finished width of the curtain. Space the tabs 4½" apart across top of curtain, ending edge of curtain with a tab. It may be necessary to increase or decrease the finished amount.

Loops may be cut from a fabric strip long enough for all the loops needed for a project, and four times the desired finished width. Turn in the two long

raw edges to meet the pressed-in lengthwise fold, then bring the two long folds together. Stitch the folds together close to the longer edge, and across the folded short end. Stitch closed to both long edges and cut into equal segments. Fold each segment in half to make a loop. Pin or baste across the raw edges. Position the raw edges of each loop so they are inserted in a seam of a project.

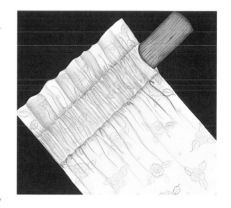

Rod-pocket curtains are often the choice when selecting a stationary window treatment that is stylish and easy to sew. Several types of rods may be used for rod-

pocket curtains, including flat rods in widths of 1", 2½", and 4½".

Unlined rod-pocket curtains can be made from sheers or laces, creating a lightweight treatment allowing filtered light into the room. For curtains made from medium-weight to heavy-weight fabrics, lining is used to make the curtains more durable, add extra body, and support the sides hems and headings.

A variety of rods are available each primarily serving a different purpose. Tension rods, used inside window frames, are held in place by the pressure of a spring inside the rod. Because mounting brackets are not used, the woodwork is not damaged by screws.

Café rods are used with or without rings. Available in several finishes, including brass and enamel, they are used for hand-drawn window treatments or tie-tab curtains.

Window hardware can be decorative as well as functional. For elaborate window treatments, traditional poles with detailed finials are available, as well as decorative tieback holders. Sleek, contemporary hardware is available for a more understated look. For a creative nontraditional look, consider using decorative knobs or other items as hardware. Rods are just as important to a window treatment as the materials. Be certain to select your desired hardware before measuring for a window treatment.

Window moldings, floors, and ceilings can be off-square, or on a slant, even in new homes. Use a carpenter's level to be certain rods are installed straight. Rods support the curtain or drapery fabric and should be level for the fabric to drape evenly.

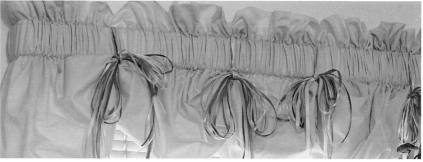

Wide curtain rods are available in both 2½" and 4½" widths. They add depth and interest to rod-pocket window treatments. Corner connectors make these rods suitable for bay and corner windows.

Sash rods use shallow mounting brackets so window treatments hang close to the glass. Available flat or round, they are commonly used for stretched curtains on doors.

Narrow curtain rods are used for rod-pocket window treatments. When sheer fabric is used, select a rod of clear or translucent plastic that will not show through the fabric.

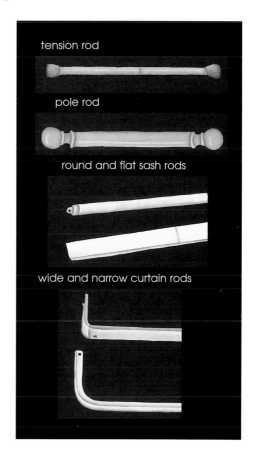

tension rod

pole rod

round and flat sash rods

wide and narrow curtain rods

For an inside mount, install hardware inside top of window frame so molding is exposed. For outside mount, install hardware at top of window frame or on the wall above the window. When hardware is mounted above the frame, visual height is added to the window treatment.

Cascades and side treatments can be mounted to cover part of the wall at the sides of the window, adding visual width. When window treatments are mounted onto the wall, more glass is exposed, letting in more light.

Whenever possible, screw brackets into wall studs. If it is necessary to position brackets between wall studs into drywall or plaster, use molly bolts to support hardware and heavy window treatments. For supporting lightweight window treatments or for installing tieback holders, plastic anchors may be used.

On brick and concrete surfaces, use masonry bolts with expanding plastic plugs. On steel or aluminum window frames, use self-drilling screws called drivers; lubricate drivers with a bar of soap for easier installation.

For long rods, or rods which will support heavy curtains, an extra bracket in the center will keep the rod from sagging. You may need an extra bracket about every four feet.

When installing rods for tab-top or café curtains preplanning is necessary. First decide how many tiers are needed. Most windows look best with two or three tiers—divide the window height into halves or thirds to install the rods. If you are dressing multipaned windows, line up the rods with the moldings that separate the glass panes. The tiers do not need to be equal; in fact, a longer tier on the bottom can make a window treatment look more balanced than when all the tiers are the same length.

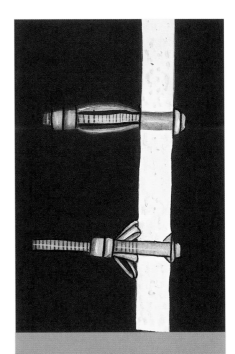

installing molly bolts

When installing molly bolts, mark your desired locations onto the wall. Using marks, drill holes for the molly bolts into the drywall or plaster. The drill-bit depends on the size of the molly bolt. Tap molly bolt into drilled hole. Tighten screw. While tightening, the molly bolt will expand, preventing it from pulling out of the wall. Remove the screw from the molly bolt, insert into hole in hardware then replace into installed molly bolt. Screw hardware securely in place.

twisted tapestries

We all know that art is not truth. Art is a lie that makes us realize truth, at least the truth that is given us to understand. The artist must know the manner whereby to convince others of the truthfulness of his lies.
— Pablo Picasso

Most houses are designed with windows architecturally placed for the aesthetic pleasure of the exterior of the home and functionally designed for the interior space. Seldom, but sometimes, the windows don't work well for the interior living space. This faux fireplace, picture, and wonderful elaborate tapestries wisely disguise the obtrusive windows while utilizing the wall space for an aesthetic end.

another greathook

No architecture is so
haughty as that which
is simple.
— John Ruskin

Sometimes simple ties or tassels are the
best solution to attaching shimmering
fabric panels to tieback hardware
mounted on the wall in place of a rod.
The design is in the hardware, not the
drapery panel, and they should not
compete with one another.

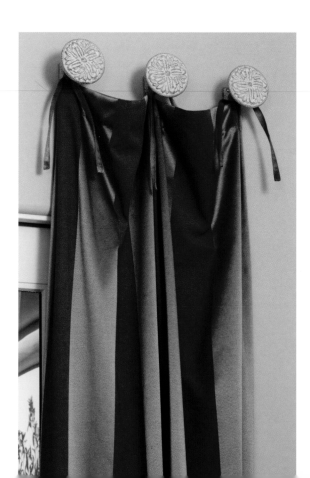

playme awindow

Great music is that which penetrates the ear with facility and leaves the memory with difficulty. Magical music never leaves the memory.
— Thomas Beecham

This trim can be changed with your mood or your tune, because it is held with only three stitches. Cut a length of fabric to the exact width of the existing drapery panel, plus 1". The width of the fabric piece should be 8"–12" depending on the size of your window and the length of the existing fabric panel. Roll the fabric lengthwise, right side out, and tuck the ends inward. Press ends flat. Gather fabric and tack onto one side of existing drapery panel, in the center and at opposite end. Pull fabric slightly apart between tacks. Repeat for each drapery panel.

little
embellishments

Life is too short to be little.
Man is never so manly as
when he feels deeply,
acts boldly, and expresses
himself with frankness and
with fervour.
— Benjamin Disraeli

Embellishing plain or printed fabrics to dramatically change the look of the drapery panel is easy as well as inexpensive.

left
Fringed tassels may be used to gather drapery panels on a wall rather than a window.

top
A decorative wall hook can be easily turned on its side and used as a tieback for window or shower curtains.

right
Chenille pom-poms are a thoughtful alternative to tassels for tiebacks. Cluster together and sew onto matching chenille cording to create one large tieback.

mechelle's half-swag

Well, nobody's perfect.
— Billy Wilder

When Mechelle created this window treatment, it happened quite by accident but ended up being very delightful. She thought she had purchased enough fabric for the window, but hadn't. Using contrasting fabrics, she knotted and nailed the materials at different heights across the window. With string, at midway, she attached the fabric to a screw and allowed the excess fabric to pool on the floor.

imperialpleasure

No man is an island entire of itself; every man is a piece of the Continent, a part of the main . . .
— John Donne

This elevated window design is effective over a single or double window. We used three lightweight scroll brackets designed to hold scarf valances, and painted them to resemble carved marble. This particular valance was made with two wide sheer scarves draped through scroll brackets. A matching tassel finished the center swag.

justonetie willdo

One half of the world cannot understand
the pleasures of the other.
— Jane Austen

We first saw this great window design in a model home in the desert of Southern California. The uncomplicated simplicity was complementary to the oriental flavor of the rest of the master bedroom.

The interior designers attached an ornamental piece of hardware traditionally used as a tieback to the wall just below the ceiling, straight up from the edge of the window (first sprayed with flat black paint). From the hardware to the window edge, they ran a piece of plastic pipe, which also had been sprayed black.

They constructed an embossed silk fabric tube using fabric glue to secure the side seams together. Using tassels attached to a decorative cord, they attached the fabric tube to the bottom of the plastic pipe, leaving a portion of the top of the tube to drape over the tasseled cording. The glued seams were hidden at the back of the tube against the wall. This is a favorite no-sew project.

24 tassels, ties, and hooks

Marni's mother-in-law disliked being alone and moved in with them. She wanted to bring some of her own things, including her bedding, which included a wonderful duvet with coordinating shams and drapery panels. The drapery panels did not fit the window; they were too long and not wide enough.

We pulled the drapery hooks from the top of the two panels and screwed a small circular hook into the wall about 6" from the ceiling and directly above each side of the window.

We purchased a small drapery tieback cord with tassels on each end and wrapped it around the top of each of the drapery panels, gathering each evenly into a circle, with the ends meeting at the side without the tassels.

After attaching each panel to a hook, with the tassels to the front, we bloused the panels on each side of the window and ballooned them at the floor.

mixandmaster

Who ran to help me when I fell,
And would some pretty story tell,
Or kiss the place to make it well?
My mother.
— Ann Taylor

one, two, three, swag

*I have hardly ever known a
mathematician who was
capable of reasoning.*
— Plato

Small arched windows often pose a dilemma, especially when they are in a large room. We were glad to see these three windows become one with the wall, due to the chosen window decor.

A decorative rod was mounted across the length of the wall. Fabric, 1½ times the desired finished width, was hemmed on both ends and draped over the rod. A small hook was attached about two-thirds of the way down the window. Fish line was wrapped around the fabric and pulled tightly. The fabric was bloused over the fish line and hook and left to droop. The wall sconces and greenery add a finishing touch to the symmetrical adaptation of this window treatment.

26 tassels, ties, and hooks

taupeambience

Elegance does not consist in putting on a new dress.
— Coco Chanel

Tassels and cords distinguish a mediocre window from an outstanding one.

right
Elongating this window and tying the tassels to create a fan above a simple fabric panel sets this one apart from the ordinary.

below
Top a roman shade with fabric flowers drawn together with decorative satin cording and tassels to add an elegant touch.

amberwaves

Be good, sweet maid,
and let who will be clever.
— Charles Kingsley

By adding different trims to a layered valance, one can create an entirely new shade. Add crisscross straps and a pressed resin medallion over a shade, or pull up slightly with a coordinating fabric peeking through from underneath. Add double tassels tied at the pull and the look of the valance is completely unique.

flavoroftheeast

Appearances often are deceiving.
— Aesop

Fabric panels can often be mounted to appear as if they can be lowered, but actually are stationary.

top
The velvet cap along the panel enhances the velvet strap trimmed with silk fringe. The little extras added to a simple roman shade make this one extraordinary.

right
The roll on this roman shade is for show and not functional. The rope, attached to two wooden balls, is a decorative faux tie which adds a third dimension to the proverbial flat shade.

I always made
an awkward bow.
— John Keats

Existing valances are easily changed with the
addition of a small amount of trim, whether it be
cording, ribbon, or another type of bauble.

above
Two simple, complementary fabric blinds, back to
back and rolled, are a wonderful addition to any
window. Simply tied with coordinating fabric strips or
ribbons gives the blinds a vertical appeal.

right
Loop a coordinating, colorful cording across an
existing valance to change the style and add a
new scalloped dimension.

lower left
Tack four matching
place mats together.
Slit holes across the
top back of each
place mat and run a
curtain rod through
the slits. Mount rod on
wall and attach rib-
bon streamers at the
top of seams.

materials & instructions

Acrylic paint to match fabric
    panels
Assorted paintbrushes
Elastic cording window width (2)
Eye screws (4)
Handkerchiefs, pressed (2)
Long tassels with cording (2)
Metal rods with hardware (2)
Panels of sheer white lace ⅘ the
    pane length plus 2" for hem
    and 2" for rod
Printed fabric panel (2)
Sewing machine
Small hooks (2)
White thread

1. Paint doors to match panels.
2. Attach rod hardware to door above glass panes. Slip panels over rods and hang.
3. Tuck a corner of the handkerchief behind rod with three corners exposed. Repeat with other glass pane.
4. Sew a 2" pocket at one end of lace panel and a 2" hem on the opposite end. Repeat with other lace panel.
5. About four-fifths of the way down, attach an eye screw on either side of the glass pane. Tie one end of the elastic cording on one eye screw. Slide lace pocket over elastic cording and secure remaining end to opposite eye screw. Repeat on other glass pane.
6. On wall beside oak trim, screw one small hook into the wall the same height as the elastic cording. Repeat on other side of wall. Tie tassel onto hook. Pull printed fabric panel to side and wrap tassel around fabric to hold in place away from door.

frenchdoorflashy

To be great is to be misunderstood.
— Ralph Waldo Emerson

This innovative concept allowed natural light to warm the room on a cold winter day by tying the privacy curtains back to the wall.

T hese window treatments may look complicated, but are quite simple.

top left

Over wooden shutter frames, we attached a simple curtain rod and hung curtain panels. A large branch, stripped of leaves, was nailed to the wall above the rod where we tied on a cotton tie-top valance. We finished by hot-gluing twigs vertically and horizontally in the shutter frames.

bottom left

Four buckskin-colored chamois were wrapped and hot-glued around the top of existing rod allowing most of them to hang down over the window. We then hot-glued a crooked willow piece over the chamois.

right

Rusty metal star hooks above the window hold a weathered, old porch post. The matching set of distressed shutters complements the color of the cotton gauze sheers draped around the post and pooled at the floor.

homespun

Junk is the ideal product . . .
the ultimate merchandise.
No sales talk necessary.
The client will crawl through
a sewer and beg to buy.
— William Burroughs

walkon thewild side

Architecture is the art
of how to waste space.
— Philip Johnson

Combining different elements
can sometimes achieve a
spectacular and unexpected
look when you are creating a
cornice. A professional made the
series of cornices, but we
thought you would be interested
to see what can be done with a
little ingenuity and a combination of materials.

The plywood was cut to fit the
windows and create the cornices. Batting was laid over the
entire front of the plywood, with
the exception of where the copper metal was going to be
placed, and adhered to the
wood with a spray adhesive.

Piping was covered to match
the fabric and sewed into the
seams of the fabric between the
front of the cornice and the
back. After being pulled over the
ends of the cornice, the fabric
was tacked down using a staple
gun at the places where the
copper was to be attached.

The copper was glued over the
fabric and the protective plastic
coating was removed. As the
copper is never touched, the fin-
ish will stay as bright as when the
copper triangle was incorporated into the cornice.

sheerprivacy

Culture, the acquainting ourselves with the best that has been known and said in the world, and thus with the history of the human spirit.
— Matthew Arnold

Sheer fabrics are as essential to light in the evening hours as they are in the daylight hours in controlling light and achieving privacy. During the day, sheers allow natural light to influence the mood of the room. After the sun goes down and the chandeliers are lit, sheers can add a dramatic ambience to a room as the light glistens and glimmers like jewels on the lacy folds of the sheer panels.

The sheers in both of these rooms were simply strung through rod pockets onto narrow, translucent curtain rods.

When used properly, sheers have the ability to create two different and unique environments, both important to our enjoyment of our surroundings.

When furnishings have been handed down from generation to generation, do not compromise their beauty with a substandard window treatment. This window deserves timeless elegance with an heirloom quality. The addition of this beautiful backdrop to the heirlooms along with the radiant silk tieback treatment, supplemented by a set of vintage sheer drapery panels, creates a time-honored tradition.

sophisticated sashes

Never explain— your friends do not need it and your enemies will not believe you anyhow.
— Elbert Hubbard

Professionally made Queen Anne valances are a sophisticated and formal window addition used to transform a simple room into an elegant chamber. By supplementing the window with a simple sheer covering, privacy is achieved without jeopardizing the light source.

There were drapery panels on this living room window. We began adding vintage laces and aged chenille throws to the decorating scheme and wanted to incorporate vintage fabrics into the window treatment. We installed a thin, lightweight rod behind the drapery rod and hung a sheer table linen over the rod. We then took a wide lace runner and draped it over the existing drapery rod, which softened the entire window and tied the room together.

lacycurtaincall

A good book is the best of friends, the same today and forever.
— Martin Tupper

To make an easy change to an existing window treatment try using vintage lace hung over an existing drapery rod and cascade it down each side of the drapes.

Only a sheer drape separates these small rooms. We removed the door to change the size of the bed from a twin to a queen. Because the door no longer opened, we tacked a decorative scarf inside the frame. Since it was sheer, we could see from room to room which also added an artistic touch.

sheerdelight

We respond to a drama to that extent to which it corresponds to our dream life.
— David Mamet

Glass block is a wonderful addition to any room where privacy is desired and natural light is essential. Draping a sheer scarf over simple hardware can warm and soften the icy contrast of a glass-block window or a large, recessed wall space.

darkside oflight

The day of the sun is like the day of a king. It is a promenade in the morning, a sitting on the throne at noon, a pageant in the evening.
— Wallace Stevens

This deeply inset window needed something to buffer the sheers without making them the focal point of the window. Two crumpled dark satin scarves allowed the light to illuminate against the fabric.

Starting at the top center of the arch, we used thumbtacks and fishing line to attach both scarves to the archway, with one scarf cascading down either side of the window. We attached the scarves again, with thumbtacks and fishing line, at the level where the arched window met the square window below and let the fabric hang naturally. We were confident a light transition had been made—no pun intended.

onthewaterfront

The marble not yet carved
can hold the form
Of every thought the greatest artist has.
— Michelangelo Buonarroti

We hung two pieces of old wrought iron, pounded to resemble snakes, at different levels. We draped etched sheer scarves over the rods and, using fish line, we tied an oriental umbrella to the end of one of the rods. The treatment romanticized an ordinary bath.

tiedinaknot

Parting is such sweet sorrow
That I shall say good night
'till it be morrow.
— William Shakespeare

It was important in this upstairs bedroom that we kept the natural light without giving up privacy. We purchased two tie-top curtains the length of the window and strung them onto a classic rod with curved finials. Using a coordinating light-colored gauze scarf, we draped it over the center of the rod so the back hung below the tab-top curtains. We tied the front piece of the scarf in a knot. We connected the two tab-top panels together at the center with a knot, completing the ensemble.

light touch

All that we see or seem Is but
a dream within a dream.
— Edgar Allan Poe

When using sheer fabrics to adorn windows, tiebacks don't always have to be touching the window trim. Experiment with tying the sheers at different places and with different materials. Ribbons can be used to tie sheers aside and, when not needed, untie easily for more privacy.

Sheers can also complement decorative glass to add privacy without giving up the decorative glass design.

weaving
somethingnew

Fanatics have their dreams,
wherewith they weave
a paradise for a sect.
— John Keats

We dressed up these vertical blinds by sponging coordinating latex paint on the slats. We then tied a knot in each end of a sheer fabric, leaving about a 12" tail and glued decorative fringe below the knot. We nailed baskets directly into the wall over the blinds and draped the sheer swag over the baskets. Purposely, we let the fabric hang unevenly on the sides for more eye appeal.

doubledensity

Window treatments can be
made easily and inexpensively.

above

Marni purchased a burlap tablecloth in Mexico. The bleached cloth
was stenciled with sunflowers and
the edges were trimmed with simple
clay beads. She combined this with
a dark burlap bag that some out-
door fencing had come in, and
made a valance for her husband's
office. She cut the tablecloth in a
24"-wide strip and nailed it above
the blind. The burlap bag was cut
into a similar strip and she tied knots
at either end. She then wound the
bag strip over and under the tablecloth to achieve the desired look.

right

We simply draped table kerchiefs
diagonally over a decorative window rod, gathering the kerchiefs
slightly to fit between the finials.

materials & instructions

Dried lavender
Dried wildflowers
Flat tin bucket with handle
Gauze fabric
Hammer & nails
Iron rack, 3-hook
Metal square with picture
Raffia
Scissors

1. Knot one corner of fabric, leaving a 6" tail. Nail through the knot in the window's corner.
2. Stretch fabric across top of window. Tie another knot and nail in the opposite corner.
3. Bring fabric to center of window, both vertically and horizontally, and tie another loose knot. Let excess hang.
4. Hang rack and bucket above one window. Decorate rack with wildflowers, lavender, and raffia. Center and hang picture above other window.

povertyposh

Resolve not to be poor:
whatever you have, spend less.
— Samuel Johnson

These window scarves were simple and inexpensive to put up, taking less than an hour to cover ordinary blinds. We didn't even hem any of the edges!

An option to knotting these sheers is the use of bracelets and napkin rings. They make great adornments when pulling sheers together.

There is always one moment in childhood
when the door opens and lets the future in.
— Graham Greene

Our friend, Julie, decided to create her own headboard. Centering the bed between two existing windows, with blinds, she went to work to create a headboard from fabric panels and silk flowers. After completing her floral masterpiece, she felt it was missing something and called us.

The headboard was attractive, but the minimal and flat window treatments were distracting. It was easily remedied, and with very little expense.

We found an old wooden frame and hung it over the drapery panels to break up the monotony of the light fabric. We purchased matching square table toppers and hung them over drapery rods. This allowed more continuity from the headboard over the windows and made the entire wall part of her creation rather than just the bed. A few more table toppers on the dark wooden night stands completed the picture.

eleganttops

Every generation revolts against its fathers
and makes friends with its grandfathers.
— Lewis Mumford

Some blinds are too impersonal. With sheer gauze fabric and silk garlands, we changed the simplicity of these blinds to more attractive windows. Using a hammer and some nails, we easily tacked the garland around and through the fabric lengths.

angels
gatherhere

The most thoughtful minds are those
which love colour the most.
— John Ruskin

Adding color and bows will brighten any little angel's room.

above

Using a fine metal wire, we attached star tulle to a white tension rod, gathering it from one side to the other. We then attached gold metal stars over the rod and the tulle.

right

This bedroom already had a balloon valance on the window. To add more color to the room, we cut several strands of multicolored 1" satin ribbons. Bunching them together, we pulled up on the valance at different intervals. We also draped gauze over the canopy bed and gathered it with the same colors of ribbons used on the valance.

silky and seethrough

Using rusty plant stakes as rods and two shades of sheer fabric, we redressed simple white blinds in this casual dining room without taking a stitch.

materials & instructions

Coordinating sheer fabrics:
    accent color (4 yds)
    main color (8 yds)
Gold acrylic paint
Hammer & nail staples
Paintbrush
Rusty metal tulip plant stakes with leaves (4)

1. Using dry paintbrush, brush gold paint over rusty metal plant stakes, leaving some rust surface exposed. Let dry.
2. Bend plant stakes to create a curvature. Nail plant stakes above windows with curvature of stake pointing outward into the room.
3. At one end, pool main colored fabric at floor, hiding cut edge under pool of fabric. Bring fabric up side of window and over first plant stake. Bend leaves and tulips to hold sheer fabric in place while looping it across the window. Be certain sheer fabric hangs low across the window opening. The sheer fabric will allow the light to enter the room.
4. Make a transition to the accent color. Pool accent fabric on floor on opposite side of window.

agedelegance

A line will take us hours maybe;
Yet if it does not seem a
moment's thought,
Our stitching and unstitching
has been naught.
— William Butler Yeats

Using crisp white table runners, we achieved a delightful window treatment in less than an hour.

materials&instructions

Board, 2x4 x width of window
Coordinating lace, window width plus 6"
Crocheted heart wreath with ribbons
Fish line
Hammer & nails
Paintbrush
Scissors
Stain matching window trim
Staple gun & staples
Table runners with lace, white (4)
Thumb tack

1. Cut one cotton table runner in half. Set aside.
2. Stain board to match window trim. Let dry.
3. Nail board to wall above window trim.
4. Staple one table runner to bottom of board with the corner of the table runner aligning with the inside corner of the window trim. The long side of the table runner should hang vertically down the window. Repeat on opposite side with another table runner.
5. Staple one table runner across the bottom of the board horizontally over the top of the vertical table runners. Attach cut edge of one half of table runner directly over the top of the vertical table runner and horizontal table runner at the corner. Repeat on other side.
6. Fold end of coordinating lace back about 1". Staple coordinating lace from wall, around end of board, across board length and around end to wall. Fold remaining lace back and attach to board against wall. Pull one-half table runner back to window trim and tack in place with staple gun. Repeat with vertical table runner.
7. Cut a piece of fish line slightly longer than the width of the horizontal table runner. Knot fish line around the heart wreath at peak. Place tack in window trim inside casing underneath horizontal table runner. Wrap other end of fish line around tack to secure.

justahintoflilac

We discovered three beautiful vintage pillowcases, which had been tucked away in a cedar chest until we came along. Two of the lacy legacies were used as accent pillows on a Victorian bed and we made a complementary window treatment with the remaining one.

materials & instructions

Iron & ironing board
Marking pen
Matching thread
Pillowcase with embroidery & lace
Rods with hardware (2)
Scissors
Sewing machine
Straight pins
Tape measure

1. Undo pillowcase at seams. Leave lace attached to both sections.
2. Attach hardware for one rod inside window below upper casing. Attach hardware for the second rod above window trim.
3. Cut one pillowcase section to fit inside window casing, allowing 1" on each side for hem and 2" at top for rod pocket. Fold sides over 1" and press in place. Using sewing machine and matching thread, stitch closed. Fold top over 2" and stitch along edge to create a pocket for the rod. Slip over rod and hang on hardware inside casing.
4. Cut other pillowcase section wide enough to cover window trim, allowing 1" on each side for hem and 2" at top for rod pocket. Shorten pillowcase section to one-third the length of the other section. Fold sides over 1" and press in place. Stitch closed. Fold top over 2" and stitch along the edge to create a pocket for the rod. Slide section over rod and hang on hardware above the window trim.

oldmother hubbard

Don't agonize. Organize.
— Florynce R. Kennedy

Look to a variety of sources for window ideas. These cupboard fabrics would make terrific curtains over a window.

To adapt this as a window treatment, simply gather the antique or vintage fabric at the top and bottom over tension rods stretched inside a window casing. Hand-painted or hand-stitched napkins can be tucked over the top of the tension rod to complete the old-fashioned adaptation.

O, Wind, If Winter comes,
can Spring be far behind?
— Percy Bysshe Shelley

winterwhiteserenity

This window had fine old woodwork so we wanted to keep it visible. We also wanted to make the window treatment blend with the landscape and not compete with the spectacular view.

We hung a simple white wooden rod across the top of the window, hung sheer cotton drapery panels with tie-tops to the rod, and tacked an old table runner from one side of the window to the other. Over the top of the table runner, we also tacked a row of vintage white lace.

The window, combined with the dainty lamp kerchief and vintage table scarf, made the room light and cozy on a warm winter's day.

French doors are normally difficult to dress. For this casual dining room we suggested the following quick and easy idea.

materials & instructions

Hammer & brads
Scissors
Sheer fabric (4 yds)
Willow place mats (2)
Willow napkin rings (2)

1. Cut the sheer fabric in half widthwise. Fold one piece into thirds lengthwise.
2. Nail fabric to top corner of windowpane with fold to the outside. Pull across windowpane and nail to other corner. Repeat on other door.
3. Nail one place mat over top of fabric. Repeat on other door.
4. Slide napkin rings over fabric panels on both doors and blouse fabric slightly above napkin rings.
5. Cut fabric diagonally below the napkin rings.

courtyardconcert

All farewells should
be sudden,
when forever.
— George Gordon Noel Byron

Metal artistry can energize a glass door and create an unparalleled window treatment.

century-old
welcome

All things are artificial,
for nature is the art of God.
— Thomas Brown

Vintage fabrics and lace, heirloom dishcloths and pillowcases, held together with old hardware clips, were layered over these door windows to achieve privacy in these cabin interiors.

bears, booties, andlace

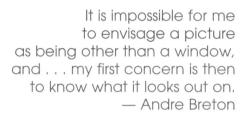

It is impossible for me
to envisage a picture
as being other than a window,
and . . . my first concern is then
to know what it looks out on.
— Andre Breton

Using sentimental objects for
tiebacks can be fun and
entertaining for children's rooms.

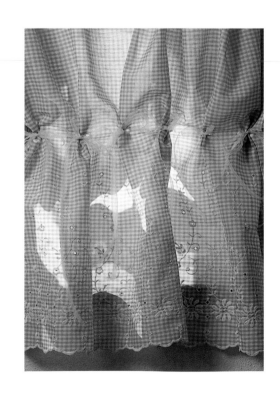

top

Heirloom baby shoes make the perfect tieback in
a new baby's room. They can easily be untied
and set aside when the curtains are closed for
naptime or nighttime.

middle

Tiny chenille bears are tied to matching swatches
with a touch of ribbon around their necks.

bottom

Ribbon laced through purple gingham eyelet
gathers nicely on a little girl's window.

quaintquilts

You may fool all the people some of the time;
you can even fool some of the people all the time;
but you can't fool all of the people all the time.
— Abraham Lincoln

The view from the window in this shower looked directly into someone else's home. To obscure the view, we used a quilt which doubled as a shower and privacy curtain.

everybloomin'thing

Always have something in sight,
even if it's just a daisy in a jelly glass.
— H. Jackson Brown, Jr.

The simplicity of a country farm kitchen cannot be matched for warmth, even when cool colors are used in the decorating scheme. These café curtains were purchased from a large department store. What sets these apart from others is the way in which they were used.

Notice the entire room is blue and white, represented in large and small patterns. The only other color presented is in the curtains; therefore, even though other patterns are more prominent, the windows stand out in the room. The fact that they are lightweight and cover only one-half to three-quarters of the window lets the sun create a warm tropical hue rather than an icy, arctic blue.

These window treatments capture the freshness of clean laundry. Heavy cotton cording was strung across the center of the windows, while an assortment of old dishcloths and embroidered items are displayed with vintage clothespins.

freshlaundry

You're only young once,
and if you work it right,
once is enough.
— Joe E. Lewis

Your descendants shall
gather your fruit.
— Publius Vergilius Maro

grandma'sheirloom

We scoured flea markets and rummage sales for the variety of patterns and colors for this window treatment. We took mismatched, inexpensive curtain rods and hung them across the bottom windowpanes. We then hung old curtain panels halfway over the rods and gathered them with different colored cloth napkins. Between the curtain panels, we hung two differing aprons.

tweetandsweet

"Hope" is the thing with feather—
That perches in the soul—
And sings the tunes without the words—
And never stops—at all—
— Emily Dickinson

Sometimes a new twist on an old rod is all you need to create a fresh look to an established window.

above
The window in this craft room needed a treatment but the room needed sunlight, so the concept for this window was easy. We hot-glued small wooden birds to the top of the metal rod after attaching the premade fabric panel to clips spaced evenly across the rod.

right
This recycled rod was embellished with drawer pulls for finials and covered with a linen and lace table runner. The drawer pulls were attached to the ends of the rod using a glue gun.

breaktheplates

One should eat to live,
not live to eat.
— Moliere

We mounted horizontal and vertical plate racks around this window. Using three rectangular tablecloths, we gathered one through each rack, tucking the ends in at the top corners.

Everything that is
beautiful and noble is
the product of reason
and calculation.
— Charles Baudelaire

Mechelle had two identical sofas in her family room, both with an attractive, but busy print. Four matching 16" pillows were on each sofa, making it hard to tell the pillows from the sofa. We took three pillows from each sofa, unzipped them, and removed the pillow forms. We stretched the pillowcases, side by side, and nailed them to the wall above the window casing. We were careful to keep the pattern on the pillowcases aligned. Using a button-attaching device, we secured two pillowcases together at the side. The third pillowcase was secured only one-third of the way down. The bottom part was opened into a vee, exposing the blinds. We secured the vee with a button-attaching device and hot-glued a jeweled button over the top.

jeansjamboree

Sometimes all a window needs is a favorite pair of old jeans.

> She gave me a smile
> I could feel in my hip pocket.
> — Raymond Chandler

above

We cut three pairs of old jeans the desired length of the valance and cut slits about 2" deep around the entire leg. By washing and drying the cut jeans, the slits curled.

Starting in the middle of the window we hung the jeans evenly across the window top. After tying the belt loops together with leather laces, we let the remaining laces hang. The treatment was finished by placing a bandanna in a pocket.

right

Using the leftover jean legs, we bunched the six jeans together over a tension rod. Then we tied bandannas around the jeans at different intervals to hold them in place.

This master bedroom had wooden blinds in a small window. We felt the window treatment should match the new tapestry and leather duvet and shams. We had no trouble finding a solid fabric to coordinate, but we had difficulty in finding a complementary pattern that would integrate with the other patterns in the shams and duvet. After making up the bed, there were two extra shams. We incorporated them into our window treatment as a header, and the combination worked fine. We left the pillow fillers in the shams before nailing them to the wall above the window. The coordinating fabric was knotted to garden hooks and pooled on the floor. The ceiling-to-floor fabric and texture elongated the window and increased the impact the window had on the room.

pillowtalk

The superfluous,
a very necessary thing.
— Voltaire

We transformed this den window with unused bedroom bedding, which added to the warmth of the rich leather furniture.

materials & instructions

Coordinating tassels on braided cord
Hammer & nails
Marking pen
Matching bed sheet
Mounting right-angle plates
Plywood to make cornice:
    width of window plus 4" x height
    from ceiling to 6" below window top
    4" x height from ceiling to 6" below
    window top (2)
Quilted bedspread to fit over plywood
Staple gun & staples
Tape measure

1. To make the cornice, nail plywood pieces together at 90 degrees.
2. Staple quilted bedspread to top and sides of cornice, overlapping excess to back. Stretch bedspread taut across front.
3. Gather and staple sheet to top of cornice. Start at end of 4" piece and work toward front center, leaving three-quarters of cornice exposed.
4. Mount right-angle plates to inside back of cornice and mount to wall, following manufacturer's instructions.
5. Tie tassels to sheet at bottom of window. Blouse bedspread slightly above tassels.

Who in the same given time
can produce more
than others has vigor,
who can produce more
and better, has talents;
who can produce
what none else can,
has genius.
— Johann Kaspar Lavater

drapedanddreamy

Susan, owner of Flora Bunda, an eclectic store in downtown Salt Lake City, always comes up with new and innovative ways to accessorize. We were utterly charmed by the awnings she made to hang inside as window treatments. One hangs on the window inside her store, the other at her home.

Fabric glue, staples, and pins keep these masterpieces together. She combined a number of elements, including silk flowers, lace, shawls, sheer fabric, ribbons, lace, and satin to establish her identity in window creativity.

ribbons ofdistinction

Variety's the very spice of life
That gives it all its flavour.
— William Cowper

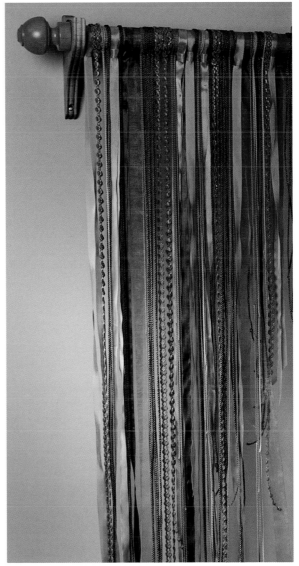

Rather than fabric, look to other embellishments for window treatments.

above
Cotton tassels were the ultimate rage in the sixties and seventies. Reinvent these tassels by stringing them on a simple metal rod over a window or doorway.

right
When fabric just won't do, try draping a multitude of colored ribbons and trims down the side of the window. The sophisticated assortment of satin ribbons may be hung by looping them over the simple wooden rod with wooden finial for a remarkable presentation that will roll with a breeze and shimmer in the light.

bygollybeads

Necessity has no law.
— Oliver Cromwell

Mechelle wanted to add something different to her basement window without spending a lot of money. We rummaged around her house and did not spend one extra dime on making this window treatment. We nailed the edge of a rectangular throw at four equal intervals, and hot-glued a drawer pull over each nail. After draping beads over the drawer pulls, leaving some dangling, we gathered the remaining throw onto the windowsill. We giggled after creating this blast from the past.

The need for comfort in small areas is a basic one.

right

To warm a tall, thin window, try a place mat. In this rock fireplace window, we hot-glued fringe to the bottom of a place mat and hammered it to the window casing with brads.

below

To liven up an ordinary shade, we hung a plant with a whimsical angel hanging from a metal curl. We also placed a large candle on a wrought-iron stand in front of the window, which did not have direct sunlight.

hangingaround

Imagination, not invention, is the supreme master of art as of life. — Joseph Conrad

vintagefloral

*I put all my genius into my life;
I put only my talent into my works.*
— Oscar Wilde

These drapes work well over a large window or as privacy curtains between rooms.

materials & instructions

Coordinating fabric
Cording
Curtain rings (every 4")
Curtain rod
Eyelets ¼"
Eyelet pliers
Fabric glue
Fusible seam tape
Iron & ironing board
Marking pen
Ribbon: ¼"-wide
Scissors
Tape measure

1. Cut panels of fabric to desired measurements. Add 7½" for hems.
2. Fold selvage edge in 1" to back side and apply fusible seam tape to fuse in place.
3. Press 2" hem on top of the panel and apply fusible seam tape.
4. Fold and adhere top hem over again.
5. Press 3½" hem on bottom and apply fusible seam tape along top edge of hem.
6. Adhere ribbon over hem to prevent fraying.
7. Mark top edge every 4" for eyelet placement. Attach eyelets on fabric.
8. Cut a 24" piece of cording for each eyelet. Thread cording through the top of each eyelet.
9. Tie drapes to rings. Place rings on curtain rod.

when
nothingbut
excesswilldo

Modernization is a fatal thing . . .
Nothing succeeds like excess.
— Oscar Wilde

fishtales

*Genius is one percent inspiration,
ninety-nine percent perspiration.*
— Thomas Alva Edison

Using an old fitted sheet, we were able to incorporate the fishing motif of this guest bedroom into the window treatment.

materials & instructions

Hammer & nails
Large rusty star hooks (2)
Plaid flannel fitted sheet
Red berries on wire garland, 5'
Twine
Wire snips
Wooden fish hung on brown twine (2 sets)

1. Nail star hooks at an angle with the hook toward the upper corner of the windows.
2. Stretch fitted sheet from one star hook to the next. Nail one side of the sheet along the top edge of the window.
3. Cut wire garland into five 12" lengths. Wrap wire garland around fitted sheet at five even intervals, gathering sheet to create balloon swags.
4. Loop twine with one section of wire garland and pull directly under swag at two different places.

windowechoes

Remembrance of things past.
— William Shakespeare

Window treatments do not always have to include fabrics. Sometimes the addition of another detail is just as effective in framing a window and a spectacular view.

above
This simple rusty metal rack hung inside the deep wooden window casing does not restrict the outside from becoming part of the inside of this home.

left
The old saw over this doorway and repeated over the mirror are a wonderful repetition, which has brought continuity from one room to the other.

offtheslopes

A taste for simplicity
cannot endure for long.
— Eugene Delacroix

We dressed this window with popular winter items. The two hooks in the top corner of the window frame hold ski poles which are lashed together to form a curtain rod for a draped woolen blanket. For the café curtain made of jeans, we ran a tension rod through the belt loops to hold them in the window.

comfortable
atmarni's

My candle burns at both ends;
It will not last the night;
But, ah, my foes, and oh, my friends—
It gives a lovely light.
— Edna St. Vincent Millay

Marni and Greg's living room had six windows of varying sizes and shapes. Their view was moderate, looking across the street into their neighbor's living room. Right after building their dream house, they purchased white wooden blinds for the lower windows so they would have immediate privacy. To dress up the rest of the window, we placed carved wooden replicas in the upper windows and fabrics, neutral in color and texture, for the drapes over the lower window blinds.

materials & instructions

Acrylic paints:
    gold
    desert suede
Carved wooden pieces (3)
Foam paintbrush
Gauze scarf panels:
    gold
    off-white
Hammer
Pencil
Rags
Rusty hooks (4)
Scissors
Screwdriver and screws
Tape measure

1. Paint wooden pieces with suede paint. Let dry.
2. Using soft rag, dust wooden pieces and rusty hooks with gold paint. Let dry.
3. Measure and mark a straight line above bottom of windows. Screw rusty hooks above window, one on each outside corner and one between each of the three windows.
4. Cut off-white panel in half. Knot each cut end. Attach a panel to the end of a rusty hook. Drape the remainder of the fabric along the sides of each window.
5. Drape gold panel across all four hooks. Keep both sides equal from the middle of the center window. Gather top of gold panel tightly, leaving bottom to hang over the window. Tie a knot in the center of the swag with the excess created from gathering the top tightly.
6. Place wooden pieces in upper windows. We did not use any means of securing these pieces for ease in dusting and window cleaning.

In helping choose fabrics to recover existing sofas and chairs, we also helped chose a coordinating drapery-weight print for this window. After deciding to create traditional pleated drapes from floor to ceiling to make the window seem larger, we were disappointed because they turned out so "ordinary." Having fabric left, we added a cornice with a slight curve that would give way to the horizontal stripes of the bookcases and vertical stripes of the drapery fabric. We also added a coordinating trim to the cornice, and glued trim along the edge of the drapes where they overlapped.

materials & instructions

Coordinating trim the length of window
Fabric glue
Fabric to cover plywood pieces
Hardware to attach plywood to wall
Iron & ironing board
Pencil
Plywood:
   width of the drapery, plus 4",
   pieces to match ends
Scissors
Spray adhesive
Staple gun & staples
Thin batting to cover one side of plywood

1. Double fabric and place cornice and ends on the wrong side of fabric. The plywood pieces that are to be extended from the wall should be placed one on each end of the large cornice. With pencil, trace the shape. Also, place individual plywood cornice and extensions on batting and trace with pencil.
2. Cut batting to exact size of plywood. Spray one side of plywood with adhesive and adhere to batting.
3. Cut fabric panels, adding 1" around all sides of fabric.
4. Turn the edge of a fabric panel in 1", matching wrong sides together. Press in place. Secure edges with fabric glue.
5. Using necessary hardware, assemble the plywood cornice together with the batting to the outside.
6. Place the other fabric panel over the batting, right side out, and pull over edges of plywood to the back. Staple in place, being careful not to stretch unevenly or cause the fabric panel to wave. Staple on the top, then the bottom, and repeat until the fabric is completely stapled around the entire cornice.
7. Attach the panel constructed in Step 4 to the inside of the cornice, securing the edges firmly with fabric glue.
8. Glue trim to drapery panel and cornice along bottom side.
9. Hang cornice and enjoy!

lettheshowbegin

Admiration.
Our polite recognition of another's
resemblance to ourselves.
— Ambrose Pierce

knoton
mywindow

One half of the world cannot
understand the pleasures of the other.
— Jane Austen

This bathroom window was dressed-
up by knotting and draping two
sheer scarves over simple hardware
around the glass blocks. The key to the
success of this window treatment is the
varied lengths of the scarves.

pictureperfect

When an interior room has no
window, create the illusion
of one. Two drapery panels
hung from rings over a rod with
decorative finials and a classic
picture over the panels also
doubles as a headboard.

Unusual window treatments double as interesting conversation pieces.

left
We found three matching woven rugs the width of the windows. Using a hammer and large-headed nails, we attached the rugs to the wall above the blinds. After rolling the rugs snugly, we secured them with raffia ties.

below
A sturdy wooden shelf was mounted above these glass doors to display collectibles.

collectibleviews

What would the world be, once bereft
Of wet and wildness?
Let them be left,
O let them be left,
wildness and wet;
Long live the weeds
and the wilderness yet.
— Gerard Manley Hopkins

ramblin' rod

*Pressed into service means
pressed out of shape.*
— Robert Frost

materials & instructions

Fabric: width of rod plus 3"
Fabric glue
Iron & ironing board
Matching thread & needle
Scissors
Tape measure

1. Lay fabric flat, right side down.
Turn edges under 1" and press.
Place fabric glue under edges
and hold in place until dry.
2. Measure circumference of rod
and add 4". Cut two pieces of
fabric to this length and 3" wide.
Fold fabric in thirds lengthwise,
wrong sides together, and press.
Fold in half widthwise and glue
ends together.
*Note: These fabric tabs will hold
the panel on the rod over the
top of the drape.*
3. Take the valance from Step 1
and pleat each end, making
small pleats. Tack pleats in place
with needle and thread. Both
ends should be pleated evenly.
4. Tack one fabric tab to back
side of pleated end.
5. Remove finials from rod ends,
slip tabs over each end and
replace finials.
6. The valance will hang slightly
lower than the drape on the
top. Gently arrange valance so
it lays evenly over drape.

This kitchen and great room connected along a long, wide wall. The kitchen was a
darker color than desired in the great room, so two different paints were used
and met at the top of the window. The stark white color of the drape created an
odd optical illusion on the wall, so an easy-to-make valance from fabric showcasing
colors from both shades of paint was added.

redress forless

A thought is often original,
though you have uttered
it a hundred times.
— Oliver Wendall Holmes

To add color to plain drapes we suggest making a dark print valance with fringe and replacing the traditional tasseled cord with a crisscross fabric ribbon glued to the back of a medallion.

materials & instructions

Decorative fabric the width of the panel plus 36" (6")
Coordinating fringe, length to match fabric, 3"–4" height
Hammer & nails
Glues:
    fabric
    wood
Scissors
Staple gun & staples
Tape measure
Wood 2x6, cut 2" longer than drapery panel width
    (1 for each panel)

1. Place the 2x6 on the 2" side. Center the decorative fabric, right side up, on the 2" side of the 2x6 and staple in place, keeping the fabric flat until you reach 3" from each end.
2. Evenly lift fabric edges and gather, stapling to the end and around the end of the 2x6.
3. Cut fringe the length of fabric panel. Adhere fringe along vertical edge of fabric with fabric glue.
4. Behind fabric topper and in front of drapery panel, nail and glue 2x6 to ceiling.

As the courtyard foliage grew around this window, it was no longer necessary to have full drapes, and the room needed more light. We shortened the existing drapes to make a new valance. We used the hemline on the bottom as our starting point and measured up to make our cut—about a quarter the length of the window. The drapery panel was lined, so we turned the lining and panel inside 1" at the cut and stitched along the right sides. We pressed it flat at the seam.

From the panel remainder, we cut six triangles, cutting through both the drape and the lining. The triangles were 2" shorter than the new valance, but when placed side by side they were the same width. We turned the lining and panel inside 1", pressed in place and sealed the seams with fabric glue. We attached a small matching tassel to the tip of each triangle.

We laid the valance on a flat surface with the triangles on top and the right side of both facing up. We tacked the triangles to the valance along the top edge.

therealskinny

A hit, a very palpable hit.
— William Shakespeare

This dining room had small corner windows, but the room needed something larger and more dramatic to go with the oversized dining table and furniture. By hanging ceiling-to-floor side panels made of heavy lined fabric on the walls at the sides of the windows, and pleating the same fabric on the walls above the window, we were able to make the windows seem much taller and wider in appearance. Structurally, the room now looked as if it could sustain the furniture the owner had intended for the room.

reachover
thetop

Two roads diverged in a wood,
and I took the one less traveled by,
And that has made all the difference.
— Robert Frost

By mounting the tieback hardware and stitched pleats directly to the drapery hardware at ceiling level, the windows seem taller and wider, and the room opened up visually. The impression of height was important in this intimate room.

glassblockreflection

Plants are always a wonderful addition to a window, especially one with a limited view. When greenery is placed in a unique and exotic plant stand, the window and objects in the window become even more charming.

Man is a creation of desire,
not a creation of need.
— Gaston Bachelard

To add more femininity to this dark, paneled room we re-covered the over-stuffed chairs and gathered a simple valance out of the same material. We took 2½ times the width of the arc in 45"-wide fabric and folded it in half lengthwise. With wrong sides together, we basted along the two edges, then pulled the threads until we achieved the width of the opening. We hot-glued the valance to the ceiling—rolling the ends under and attaching them above the drapery panel. Finally we pulled the fabric apart, creating a rounded, balloon appearance.

flipoverthetop

I do not ask you much.
— William Shakespeare

Sometimes the simple task of draping fabric over a rod is all one needs to create a new twist to an old window covering.

above
Pinched pleats with a tailored hemline are certainly the answer to giving a simple swag a sophisticated look. The coordinating fabrics tie the decorative elements of the room together nicely.

right
Draped over a simple brass rod, this dainty panel valance is accentuated by delicate embroidery and tiny pom-pom trim. It is the perfect layer over the sheer and lacy drapery panel pooling at the floor.

drapesinrow

Give me a look, give me a face,
That makes simplicity a grace.
— Ben Jonson

Replace a long rod that spans the entire width of a window with individual panel rods to create a refreshing and contemporary approach to framing a window.

vibrantpanels

Safe upon the solid rock
the ugly houses stand:
Come and see my shining palaces
built upon the sand.
— Edna St. Vincent Millay

Using more panels than is necessary
for privacy can stimulate a window
and a room.

above

This window covering was made with panels of hand-painted fabrics and prestrung beaded trim. Two rods were used to hang the curtains. The sheer curtains were hung on the front rod and the heavier cotton or velvet curtains were hung on the second rod.

left

Several inches have been added into the length of these drapes so they puddle on the floor. These drapes are adorned with beaded tassels. Also, there is a mixture of sheet and opaque fabrics so one can spread out the sheer panels and let the light through, or scrunch the sheer panels and spread out the opaque panels for privacy.

all dressed up 93

soulshelves

Be a good animal,
true to your animal instincts.
— D. H. Lawrence

Reproductions of antique metal have become quite popular and can be easily added as a window treatment.

above
This shelf was the exact width of the window. It was lightweight, so we nailed it above the window. We topped the shelf with a variety of aromatic candles, some in exotic animal prints which coordinated with the existing bed linens.

right
Architectural stars such as these can be displayed around a doorway or windowpane.

firstimpressions

We added personality and depth to these wooden blinds with simple doorknobs and vintage tins. We nailed wall hangers to the back of doorknobs, still on a part of the original door. We nailed the wood on either side of the window top and nailed tins between the wood, overlapping the tins to fit the space. To complete the window treatment, we draped a scarf over each doorknob with one side of the scarf shorter than the other.

iron
curves

When a work appears to
be ahead of its time,
it is only the time that is
behind the work.
— Jean Cocteau

Consider something
other than tradition-
al straight rods. These
scroll-worked and curl-
angled iron rods are as
important to the win-
dow treatment as the
fabrics and tassels.

right
Finials can be adapted to replace a rod. These four were mounted in the ceiling and the tie-top drapery panels were hung directly on the decorative finials.

top
To add separation between this dining area and living room, we attached eye screws directly in the wooden frames of vintage windows. With leather shoelaces, we hung antique leaded-glass windows from rusty garden hooks turned on their side and secured to the ceiling.

heavy metal 97

And indeed there will be time
To wonder, "Do I dare?" and, "Do I dare?"
Time to turn back and descend the stair,
With a bald spot in the middle of my hair . . .
Do I dare disturb the universe?
— T. S. Eliot

paintedmetalmagic

This dining area had double doors flanked by a window on either side. There were white wooden blinds on the windows and honeycomb shades on the doors. Using items from a local craft store, we embellished the windows and doors to make them whole.

materials & instructions

Aqua blue oxidizer
Clear matte sealer
Hammer & nails
Hot-glue gun & glue sticks
Large rusty metal star
Lightweight craft copper, 8"-wide (3')
Metal snips
Rusty metal reindeer, (2)
Scissors
Small rusty plant stakes, (8)
Sponge brush
White sheer gauze fabric the length of the window
Willow branches (4 packages)

1. Tie a knot in one corner of gauze. Nail gauze at upper left corner of window, hiding the nail with the knot. Pull gauze across window and knot at other corner. Nail and conceal nail with knot. Repeat on other window.
2. Pull fabric to a vee in the center of the window and tie a knot in the gauze. Repeat on other window.
3. Cut three pieces of copper approximately 8" x 12".
4. Using sponge brush, apply aqua blue oxidizer to each piece of copper. Let dry about one hour. Apply clear sealer so color won't wipe off. Let dry.
5. Arch copper pieces slightly forward. Nail one piece to the center of the window. Allow space between wall and copper to insert branches. Repeat for each window.
6. Insert desired number of willow branches into each end of copper pieces. Bend stake ends of stars and insert in ends of copper pieces.
7. Hot-glue rusty star to copper piece at center. Adhere metal reindeer to copper pieces above windows.

make
mine metal

When we build,
let us think that we build forever.
— John Ruskin

Suggested for small window openings,
metal and wrought iron are fabulous
decorative additions. Mounted within a
window or around a window, they create
an unusual visual pattern as well as act as
security against unwanted entry.

patchwork glass

And is it true? And is it true,
This most tremendous tale of all,
Seen in a stained-glass window's hue . . .
— John Betjeman

Sometimes no window covering is necessary, even in an intimate room. The movable screen allows privacy, yet allows the warmth of the sun to light the room.

Colored or textured glass is the epitome of a window as interpretive art. There is nothing else needed to make a statement, either formally or casually.

heavy metal 101

Thy decay Is still impregnate with divinity.
— George Gordon Noel Byron

This wonderful old wooden screen door can be used to frame a small window with a café curtain. It also can easily hang alone as a charming addition to any room. This is a new look at old hardware at its very best.

today a mirror,
tomorrow . . . it could be a window

starting over

For the world has lost
his youth,
and the times
begin to wax old.
— Apocrypha

104 hard side of windows

Old windows are terrific accent accessories to use on walls. They are sensational alone, but you may add dried flowers, photographs, or pictures for variety. Our favorite old window idea is to use one as a frame for photographs, which can be changed readily because removable tape is used to secure the photographs to the back of the glass.

happytrails

The best part of the art of living is to
know how to grow old gracefully.
— Eric Hoffer

Adding some classic Western
memorabilia, coupled with dried
flowers gathered from a Wyoming
landscape, to this turn-of-the-century
screen door brings energy to a plain
pine-covered wall.

   If a western motif is not what you
are looking for, try using a vintage
door as a backdrop for a different
time period.

bundlesoftrim

A friend may well be reckoned
the masterpiece of Nature.
— Ralph Waldo Emerson

It used to be that college students and
newlyweds were the only ones who
could get away with hanging a simple
piece of fabric for blinds over a window
for privacy, and topped it with sprigs of
willows wrapped in twine. Now it is chic.

Willows whiten, aspens quiver,
Little breezes dusk and shiver.
— Alfred Tennyson

endofthetrail

We tried three different looks on this window to show there is not just one right way to trim a rustic window.

top
We decoupaged colorful, pressed autumn leaves onto a painted peg board. After nailing it to the window frame, we tied a raffia bundle around each peg, allowing them to hang down over the window.

middle
We hammered a long nail into the corner of the window frame and hung a stirrup, lariat, and an old cowboy hat over the edge of the casing.

bottom
Using a hammer and 3" nails in each corner of the window frame, we attached a holiday garland over the nails, winding the vine of garland around the nails to secure it.

nature'sgarden

God Almighty first planted a garden. And indeed, it is the purest of human pleasures.
— Francis Bacon

The key to making these delightful windows is creating them with objects you like to see over and over again. Whether you screw a rack above the window and hang dried flowers, baskets on the pegs, or string pussy willows through mounted antlers that have been shed, you can bring nature indoors.

A combination of window treatments is oftentimes appealing and stimulates a room. Each element, which could very successfully stand alone, should complement, not compete.

below
Combine a single wreath with shutters, stained glass, and laced tiebacks for a winning combination.

above
Remove the clutter and repeat with the simplicity of grapevine wreaths for a down-to-earth splash of nature to accentuate a series of windows.

above
Come back to basics with antlers mounted on a simple painted peg board adorned with tied willows.

heartfeltwelcome

The call of the wild.
— Jack London

Look to nature for an inexpensive and unique window treatment.

above

Cut a grapevine wreath into sections and pull apart. Staple above window. Wind silk garland through grapevines. Incorporate additional silk leaves for more color.

above center

Tie bundles of branches together with wire. The length of the branches need to be proportionate to the size of the window. Tie the two bundles together, creating a right angle, and place above the window using a hammer and nail.

left

Hang a willow heart over metal blinds for a seasonal twist. Be certain wreath does not interfere with the function of the existing hardware.

autumnclassic

No spring, nor summer beauty hath such grace,
As I have seen in one autumnal face.
— John Donne

We purchased some great handmade paper with leaves and ripped the edges so they fit the height and width of our windows. We tacked the paper directly to the window trim using small brads. We then hot-glued some autumn leaves onto the bottom border. We purchased the leaves, but it would be fun to collect, press, and use your own.

down
todetail

And so our mothers and grandmothers have, more often than not anonymously, handed on the creative spark.
— Alice Walker

W hile some relish simplicity, others lavish in excess when dressing their windows.

above
Linda's mother, Margene, trims her living room swags seasonally. This Christmas adornment was one of our favorites.

left
Mechelle's mother, Joan, painted this attractive border across the ceiling and chair molding. She purchased the soft white patterned satin drapery scarf with corner rosettes and hung it over the window behind the bed.

We suggested that a little color might add the finishing touch to the ensemble. Sheer 2"-wide ribbon, in a soft pastel purple, was used to cascade down the white scarf from the rosettes gathered at each corner.

practicingsimplicity

Hip is the sophistications
of the wise primitive
in a giant jungle.
— Norman Mailer

Wreaths are a popular
and inexpensive way
to decorate. They can be
purchased or easily con-
structed using a variety of
different materials.

let the sunshine in

God's first creature,
which was light.
— Francis Bacon

This is a perfect valance to let the sun shine in. These twisted branches were wired together to create a rod, and laid over wrought iron hardware mounted to the wall at each corner of the window. A cotton sheer scarf was draped around, over, and through the limbs, hanging down evenly on each side of the window. We kept the color neutral because we wanted to maintain the simplicity of the room. The object was to add a texture and new dimension without interfering with the view.

woodand
windows

I sprang to the stirrup,
and Joris, and he;
I galloped, Dirk galloped,
we galloped all three.
— Robert Browning

This bathroom needed some privacy but also a natural light source. We made four frames, which fit inside the window casing. We cut red willow branches to fit inside the frames on a diagonal. A small amount of wood glue held them in place. Shutter hardware was used to attach two pairs together before mounting, one set to each side of the wall. They were raised slightly above the windowsill for freedom of movement.

Consider removable metal decals to add variety to shutter tops.

magicalmixes

They are ill discoverers that think there is no land,
when they can see nothing but sea.
— Francis Bacon

Bamboo or rattan blinds are inexpensive and require little maintenance. We suggested woven blinds for this room because of the existing furnishings and floor covering. The repetition of the woven blinds on the multiple windows worked well with the repetition of the patterned floor covering and simple woven rug under the coffee table. The simplicity of the window coverings did not conflict with the dual prints on the overstuffed chair and ottoman or the decorative chest of drawers.

Between good sense and good taste
there lies the difference between
a cause and its effect.
— Jean de La Bruyere

glassartistry

A n antique beveled window in its original wooden frame is a wonderful
window treatment. Whether hung by a
chain or a grosgrain ribbon, the bevels of
the glass create a rainbow palette of
color, especially against the light of a
silent flame or sunny window.

A contemporary glass creation can oftentimes be a great room divider, especially from a dimly lit room to one with substantial light. The glass lets natural light filter through, creating a warm glow during daylight hours. It also allows an enchanting reflection in the evening hours.

don'tfencemein

And now for something
completely different.
— Monty Python's Flying Circus

Don't ever miss an opportunity to purchase a piece of an old ceiling tile because the uses are endless. These two lightweight tiles were nailed above the window at the ceiling height, covering the top of the window. The fringe was hot-glued to the back of the tiles. The combination of the hard surface and soft texture of the trim came together to create a whole. A wooden blind for privacy is hidden behind the ceiling tiles.

olddoors fornew windows

Life begins at forty.
— Walter B. Pitkin

While rummaging through the attic of an old stable, we came across these wonderful carved Mexican doors. The curvature on the top of the doors was very similar to the arch on the top of this new living room window. Hung with some strong, contemporary brass door hinges, we attached them to the sides of the windows just as we would to a door frame. This made a unique addition to the vintage trunk, also found stashed in the stable.

littlewrangler

The "good old times"—
all times when old are good.
— George Gordon Noel Byron

These western windows use an eclectic combination of finds to add personality to these rooms.

left
The blue plaid cotton dish towels are gathered in the center with a tasseled cord. The large sisal ropes tie back the curtains on the outside of the bay window. Four embroidered pillowcases, trimmed with gold tassels, hang over heavy twine, creating the privacy curtain at the window bottom. The antique oxen yoke, hung at wall level, finishes this living-room display.

right
Winning ribbons, a saddle, ropes, and other horse memorabilia adorn this little wrangler's bedroom.

A horse! A horse!
My kingdom for a horse!
— William Shakespeare

Old hooks, spurs, and horseshoes make perfect hardware for adding a rustic look to a simple window.

below
Large vintage hooks were used to hang this replica of an Indian spear above an arena window. The antique leather fly net, once used to keep the flies off horses, is also a creative addition to the window.

right
We found that spurs were just the right size to hold these lodge poles and tie-top drapery panels.

bootsandbuffaloes

Never confuse movement with action.
— Ernest Hemingway

Wall sculpture added to a window is a wonderful focal point in a room.

materials & instructions

Baskets with handles (2)
Copper paint
Craft knife
Hammer & nails
Lightweight wire
Rusty metal wall sculpture
Paintbrush
Pussy willows (2 bundles)

1. Paint blind header with copper. Let dry.
2. Cut one handle off the right side of a basket. Cut one handle off the left side of the other basket.
3. Wire pussy willow bundles to the header, keeping the ends out.
4. Nail baskets to the center of the window above the header and over the pussy willow bundles.
5. Wire wall sculpture over the top of the baskets.

The only thing that separates us
from the animals is our ability to accessorize.
— Robert Harling

When Dave and Linda added a pond on their ranch, they named the pond after their first labrador, Boomer. They were given a wonderful sign with Boomer's name painted on it, giving it a personal touch. A small cabin, erected in the late 1880s, was moved and reerected near the new pond. They hung the sign over the sliding glass doors of the cabin, which led to the deck on the pond, and added a few cattails, which were dried and dipped in polyurethane for preservation, to one side of the sign. The addition of the sign above the window personalized the room.

ride'emcowboy

Time for a little something.
— A. A. Milne

The Durbanos built an indoor arena with an upstairs apartment that overlooked the riding area. There was no need to cover the windows in the living-room area because no one would be looking in after hours.

Linda found some wonderful old metal ceiling tiles, bowed them slightly out, and nailed one above each of the four windows, leaving a gap at each end. She gathered willow branches after the leaves had already fallen, bundled them together, and stuck the bundles in each of the ends of the ceiling tiles. The tiles drew the observer to the window without distracting from what was going on in the arena.

highcountry
valance

Both of these valances were made with a 2' section of 6'-wide willow fencing.

above
Dried flowers woven through the fencing slats dressed up this valance.

right
Silk leaves with berries attached with soft-gauge wire brought a softer look into this room.

workingwithwood

W ood is a wonderful addition as a window treatment. We felt these were some you do not ordinarily see.

Rather than glass, adding small twigs to this shutter frame brought a Southwest flavor to the room.

This throw rug is hung vertically over the door panes for privacy. The doors act as a buffer between the dining room and kitchen at the Old Corral Steakhouse in Centennial, Wyoming.

This multicolored rug was stapled to a decorative quilt rack and nailed above the existing blinds.

rustic regal 133

inanutshell

Look with favor on a bold enterprise.
— Virgil

This simple window treatment has three elements that make it stand out from the rest: the finials, the tieback, and the fabric. For privacy the tieback can easily be removed.

materials & instructions

Complete acorn shells (12)
Drawer pulls (2)
Drill with bit slightly larger than wire
Hot-glue gun & glue sticks
Leather the size of the window
Medium-gauge wire, 6"-dia. circle
Metal rod with hardware
Pliers

1. Using pliers, pull ends off rod. Twist screws into drawer pulls. Place hot glue in one end of rod. Put screw into end of rod so drawer pull is flush with rod. Hold in place until glue dries. Repeat at other end of rod.
2. Hang rod hardware on wall, following manufacturer's instructions.
3. Hot-glue leather over rod, leaving an opening large enough to slide over drawer pulls.
4. Hang rod on hardware.
5. Drill two small holes on opposite sides of each acorn. String them on wire and bend into a 6" circle. Twist wire closed with pliers. Slide acorn wire over the bottom of leather.

makingan entrance

One might well say that mankind is divisible into two great classes: hosts and guests.
— Max Beerbohm

When two windows are visible from adjoining rooms, it is not necessary that they match, but their window treatments should coordinate.

The rich wood in these rooms made it easy to add a number of different patterns and textures to the windows.

The dining area looked great with a white cotton drape, but we wanted something more dramatic in the sitting room. We found two blankets that coordinated with the tapestries in the room. We mounted a simple wooden rod across the large window and adjoining door that led outside. We attached one of the blankets to the wooden hardware with fish line and let it hang. Then we looped the other blanket over the top of the rod for a colorful, rustic window dressing.

stackedpretty

There is a garden in her face
Where roses and white lilies grow;
A heavenly paradise is that place
Wherein all pleasant fruits do flow.
— Thomas Campion

Wonderful painted benches, stacked in front of a window with no view, make great shelves for dried flower arrangements of all sizes, colors, and textures.

picturepriority

When the window doesn't have a view or a great light source, feel free to block the window, treat it as a wall, and accessorize in front of it.

Drapery panels can successfully be used to frame memorabilia and accessories.

justfortheholidays

If we do not find anything very pleasant, at least we shall find something new.
— Voltaire

Just for the Christmas holidays we replaced existing window treatments with holiday coverings.

above
We removed traditional holiday ornaments from this pinecone garland, added some baby's breath, and glued on a few acorns before wiring it above vertical blinds.

left
Paint is a marvelous medium for windows and is easily and inexpensively changed from season to season. This colorful way lets the light shine in from a window with a poor view.

lower left
Table runners were folded over the top of this existing rod and hot-glued together. Small ornaments with satin ribbon were then glued to the tips of the runners.

holiday
simplicity

Art is man's expression
of his joy in labour.
— William Morris

We placed a sheer
fabric backdrop
between the Christmas
tree and the front win-
dow. The fabric illumi-
nated from inside out,
while blocking the
competition from out-
door holiday lights.

changetheview
withsheerandilluminating
windowcoverings

disguise a small window with an entire wall of fabric

rooms without a view

A dash of color in a room can often compensate when there is no view.

above

These half-blinds over tall windows keep the upper portion open as a light source without compromising necessary privacy. For simplicity, we chose a more contemporary, smooth draped fabric. However, this concept could easily be enhanced by using a gathered or pleated fabric to give the windows a different dimension.

right

In a small space, a window ledge may be used to showcase treasures or works of art.

metricconversionchart

INCHES	MM	CM	INCHES	CM	INCHES	CM
⅛	3	0.3	9	22.9	30	76.2
¼	6	0.6	10	25.4	31	78.7
½	13	1.3	12	30.5	33	83.8
⅝	16	1.6	13	33.0	34	86.4
¾	19	1.9	14	35.6	35	88.9
⅞	22	2.2	15	38.1	36	91.4
1	25	2.5	16	40.6	37	94.0
1¼	32	3.2	17	43.2	38	96.5
1½	38	3.8	18	45.7	39	99.1
1¾	44	4.4	19	48.3	40	101.6
2	51	5.1	20	50.8	41	104.1
2½	64	6.4	21	53.3	42	106.7
3	76	7.6	22	55.9	43	109.2
3½	89	8.9	23	58.4	44	111.8
4	102	10.2	24	61.0	45	114.3
4½	114	11.4	25	63.5	46	116.8
5	127	12.7	26	66.0	47	119.4
6	152	15.2	27	68.6	48	121.9
7	178	17.8	28	71.1	49	124.5
8	203	20.3	29	73.7	50	127.0

The end may justify the means
as long as there is something
that justifies the end.
— Leon Trotsky